TORONTO MAPLE

DEDICATION

All rights reserved. Neither this book nor any portion thereof may be reproduced or used in any manner whatsoever without the express written permission.

Disclaimer: The following book is for entertainment and informational purposes only. The information presented is without contract or any type of guarantee assurance. While every caution has been taken to provide accurate and current information, it is solely the reader's responsibility to check all information contained in this article before relying upon it. Neither the author nor publisher can be held accountable for any errors or omissions. Under no circumstances will any legal responsibility or blame be held against the author or publisher for any reparation, damages, or monetary loss due to the information presented, either directly or indirectly. This book is not intended as legal or medical advice. If any such specialized advice is needed, seek a qualified individual for help.

Trademarks are used without permission. Use of the trademark is not authorized by, associated with, or sponsored by the trademark owners. All trademarks and brands used within this book are used with no intent to infringe on the trademark owners and only used for clarifying purposes.

CONTENTS

QUESTIONS 1 5

QUESTIONS 2 7

QUESTIONS 3 9

QUESTIONS 4 11

QUESTIONS 5 13

QUESTIONS 6 15

QUESTIONS 7 17

QUESTIONS 8 19

QUESTIONS 9 21

QUESTIONS 10 23

QUESTIONS 11 25

QUESTIONS 12 27

QUESTIONS 13 29

QUESTIONS 14 31

QUESTIONS 15 33

QUESTIONS 16...35

QUESTIONS 1

1. Which Leafs goalie was nicknamed "The China Wall"?
2. Which San Jose player did Toronto acquire for their 2003 post-season run in exchange for Brad Boyes, Alyn McCauley, and a 1st round choice?
3. No one is more closely associated with Leafs failure than Harold Ballard, the team's majority owner from 1972 until his death in 1990. Which of the following describes Ballard?
4. Mats Sundin played with the Maple Leafs from 1994 to 2008, scoring 420 regular season goals. Whose Maple Leaf team record of 389 goals did Sundin eclipse during the 2007-08 season?
5. The Leafs defeated the Detroit Red Wings 4-3 in game seven of the first round of the 1993 NHL playoffs. Name the four Leaf goal scorers from that game.
6. Who did the Leafs take with their first pick in 1995?
7. What was Jack Adams's nickname?
8. Who was Ed Belfour's first team?
9. The first Toronto N.H.L. team to win the Stanley Cup had which nickname?
10. Who was suspended for eight season games and some playoff games for elbowing Scott Niedermeyer?

ANSWERS 1

1. Johnny Bower
2. Owen Nolan
3. He was a convicted felon.
4. Darryl Sittler
5. Glenn Anderson, Bob Rouse, Doug Gilmour, Nikolai Borschevsky
6. Jeff Ware
7. Jolly Jack
8. Chicago Blackhawks
9. Arenas
10. Tie Domi

QUESTIONS 2

1. What is the nickname of Bill Barilko, who played 5 seasons for Toronto in the late 40s and early 50s?
2. Doug Gilmour wore number 93 for the Toronto Maple Leafs. Which of the following Leafs also wore that number?
3. Which of these years was the last time the Maple Leafs brought home the Cup during the 20th century?
4. Which Leafs player won the MVP in 1955?
5. In 2010, Jason Blake and Vesa Toskala, two players seen as under-performers with heavy contracts, were traded to Anaheim for this goalie. Who is he?
6. In 1973, the Leafs acquired goalie Doug Favell and a first round draft pick in a trade with the Philadelphia Flyers. Who did Leafs give up for these assets?
7. Hall of Famer Johnny Bower was a member of the Maple Leafs from 1958 to 1970. Which position did Bower play?
8. Which Maple Leaf scored his first NHL goal in his first NHL game, during the last game of the regular season for the 2002-2003 season?
9. Who did the Leafs take with their first pick in 1996?
10. What was Claire Alexander's nickname?

ANSWERS 2

1. Bashin Bill
2. Alexander Godynyuk
3. 1967
4. Ted Kennedy
5. Jean-Sebastian Giguere
6. Bernie Parent
7. Goalie
8. Matt Stajan
9. Marek Posmyk
10. The Milkman

QUESTIONS 3

1. In what year did Mats Sundin become captain of the Maple Leafs?
2. Which one of these Leafs was the last to lead the league in scoring?
3. Which former Leafs player was referred to in the Mike Myers movie 'Austin Powers'?
4. What nickname was associated with Andy Bathgate?
5. How many Toronto Maple Leafs players are in the Hockey Hall of Fame, ending with the 2001 season?
6. How many jerseys did Leafs retire in the 20th century?
7. Who was the first player from Europe to join the Leafs?
8. In 2008, which Leaf fan favourite was traded to the Florida Panthers for a 5th round draft pick?
9. In the middle of the 1979-80 season, dynamic forward Lanny MacDonald was traded from the Leafs to the Colorado Rockies. What was the fallout from the trade?
10. Dave Keon was an outstanding center for the Maple Leafs from 1960 to 1975. Which uniform number did Keon wear for most of his career?

ANSWERS 3

1. 1997
2. Gordie Drillon
3. Doug Gilmour
4. Handy Andy
5. 34
6. 2
7. Inge Hammarstrom
8. Wade Belak
9. Captain Darryl Sittler tore the C off his sweater.
10. 14

QUESTIONS 4

1. You were in Maple Leaf Gardens in 1998, and your seats were right behind the boards. What colour were your seats?
2. Who did the Leafs take with their first pick in 1997?
3. What was Mike Allison's nickname?
4. What year was it when Mats Sundin got traded to the Leafs?
5. Who was the first Leaf to win the Conn Smythe trophy?
6. Who wore number 39 on his jersey in 2002?
7. George Armstrong played his entire career of 21 season with the Leafs. What was his nickname?
8. How many team names has the Toronto Franchise had in the 20th Century?
9. What round pick was Curtis Joseph drafted?
10. This Calder winning goalie was acquired from Boston in exchange for the rights to a prospect named Tukka Rask. Who is this goalie?

ANSWERS 4

1. Gold
2. Jeff Farkas
3. Red Dog
4. 1994
5. Dave Keon
6. Travis Green
7. Chief
8. 3
9. 1st
10. Andrew Raycroft

QUESTIONS 5

1. Which of the following accurately describes the Toronto Maple Leafs of the 1980s?
2. This Swedish-born defenseman played for the Maple Leafs from 1973 to 1989, scoring over 100 goals in his years with Toronto. Can you name him?
3. Who scored the winning goal in overtime in game three of the 2001 playoff series against Ottawa?
4. Who did the Leafs take with their first pick in 1998?
5. What was Glenn Anderson's nickname?
6. What number was the Maple Leaf's right winger Tom Fitzgerald in 2002?
7. Which of the following players has never been captain of the Toronto Maple Leafs?
8. Of these Leafs players, who plays both defense and offense?
9. Allan Bester, one of the younger Toronto goalies to don the Leaf jersey, what was his nickname?
10. Who was the head coach of The St. John's Maple Leafs (Farm Team) in of 1999?

ANSWERS 5

1. They did not have a single winning season.

2. Borje Salming

3. Cory Cross

4. Nikolai Antropov

5. Andy

6. 12

7. Tim Horton

8. Wade Belak

9. The Beast

10. Al MacAdam

QUESTIONS 6

1. Who scored the last goal at Maple Leaf Gardens?
2. I was drafted from the Philadelphia Flyers in 2007. I played for 6 seasons until I was traded to the Toronto Maple Leafs. Who am I?
3. Expressing his feelings of being uncomfortable in the environment of the Toronto Maple Leafs, Kris Versteeg requested a trade and was sent to Philadelphia in 2011 for a 1st and 3rd round draft pick in the 2011 draft. What prospects did the draft picks end up becoming?
4. After the 1987-88 season, the Leafs hired Gord Stellick as general manager. What distinguished Stellick?
5. During the 1967-68 season, the Maple Leafs traded superstar forward Frank Mahovlich to the Detroit Red Wings for which star center?
6. Mike Gartner was traded from New York to Toronto during the 1993-1994 season. Who was the principal player who went to New York in that deal?
7. Who did the Leafs take with their first pick in 1999?
8. What was Lloyd Andrews's nickname?
9. Where was Maple Leaf's, Aki Berg born?
10. Only once in their history have the Toronto Maple Leafs had the number one pick in the entry draft. Whom did they select?

ANSWERS 6

1. Bob Probert

2. James Van Riemsdyk

3. Stuart Percy, Josh Leivo

4. He was the youngest GM in the history of the league.

5. Norm Ullman

6. Glenn Anderson

7. Luca Cereda

8. Shrimp

9. Finland

10. Wendel Clark

QUESTIONS 7

1. Which player was the Leafs' first round pick in the draft of 2000?
2. Nikolai Borschevsky was one of the grinders on the team at the time. What was his nickname?
3. When was the last time in the 20th century that the Toronto Maple Leafs failed at the last hurdle, to go to the Stanley Cup finals to face the Montreal Canadiens?
4. How many NHL teams has Wendel Clark played for?
5. Who was replaced by Turk Broda in 1936?
6. In 2002, this solid defenseman was traded to Florida in exchange for the rights to Robert Svehla. Who is this defenseman?
7. On February 13, 1999, the Leafs played their last game at Maple Leaf Gardens, their home arena for 68 seasons and 11 Stanley Cup championships. Which Leafs alumnus was conspicuously absent from the commemorative ceremony?
8. Tim Horton was a star player with the Maple Leafs from 1949 to 1970. Which one of these statements about Horton is true?
9. Who scored late in game six of the Leafs' first round series against Philadelphia in 1999, to give the Leafs a 1-0 victory and 4-2 series victory?
10. Who did the Leafs take with their first pick in 2000?

ANSWERS 7

1. Brad Boyes

2. Nick the Stick

3. 1992-1993

4. 6

5. George Hainsworth

6. Dmitri Yushkevich

7. Dave Keon

8. He was an All-Star defenseman

9. Sergei Berezin

10. Brad Boyes

QUESTIONS 8

1. What was Dave Andreychuk's nickname?

2. Who were the two assistant coaches for the Toronto Maple Leafs in 2002?

3. What team traded Paul Henderson to Toronto?

4. Pat Boutette in my mind was one of Toronto's most dedicated players. What was his nickname?

5. When was the last game at Maple Leaf Gardens played?

6. How many Stanley Cups did the Leafs win during the 20th century?

7. Who had the nickname "Chief"?

8. Acquired alongside Dion Phaneuf and Fredrik Sjostrom in 2010 for Jamal Mayers, Ian White, Niklas Hagman, and Matt Stajan, which defenseman prospect played some good minutes in Toronto but was ultimately shipped to Tampa Bay in a future trade?

9. In the 2005 off-season, the Leafs sought to bolster the lineup by signing a high-profile free agent to a one year contract. Who was it?

10. Walter Broda was a legendary goalie for the Maple Leafs from 1936 to 1951. What was Broda's popular nickname?

ANSWERS 8

1. Chuckie

2. Rick Ley and Keith Acton

3. Detroit Red Wings

4. Bash

5. February 13th, 1999

6. 13

7. George Armstrong

8. Keith Aulie

9. Eric Lindros

10. Turk

QUESTIONS 9

1. Who was the principal Leaf going to Buffalo in exchange for Dave Andreychuk in the February 1993 trade?
2. Who did the Leafs take with their first pick in 2001?
3. What was Syl Apps's nickname?
4. When was the last time the Leafs won the Cup in the 20th century?
5. What Toronto goalie was forced to leave a 1972 playoff game, when New York Ranger tough guy Vic Hadfield threw his mask into the stands at Madison Square Garden during a brawl?
6. Celebrated Toronto goalie Johnny Bower was given what nickname?
7. What team was the second last to play at Maple Leaf Gardens, and second to play at Air Canada Centre?
8. In what year were the Maple Leafs 'born'?
9. Which Leafs goalie surpassed Terry Sawchuk in wins?
10. As a symbol of loyalty and respect for an iconic player on their team, which declining all-star was traded to Toronto in 2004 for a modest 4th round draft pick; because Toronto offered a much bigger opportunity for him to go after the Stanley Cup?

ANSWERS 9

1. Grant Fuhr

2. Carlo Colaiacovo

3. Slippery Syl

4. 1967

5. Bernie Parent

6. The China Wall

7. Carolina Hurricanes

8. 1927

9. Ed Belfour

10. Ron Francis

QUESTIONS 10

1. After a seven year absence, the Leafs qualified for the playoffs in 2013 and were eliminated in the 1st round in seven games by the Boston Bruins. What happened in game seven?

2. This center played his entire NHL career (1949-71) with the Maple Leafs, scoring 296 goals with Toronto. He was nicknamed "The Chief". Can you identify this member of the Hall of Fame?

3. Where did Toronto Maple Leafs forward Darcy Tucker play his junior hockey?

4. Who did the Leafs take with their first pick in 2002?

5. What was Al Arbour's nickname?

6. Who was the captain for the Maple Leafs in 1945?

7. Which Swedish winger joined the Leafs in 1973 along with star defenceman Borje Salming, paving the way for a flood of Europeans into the NHL?

8. Longtime Toronto goalie Walter Broda was given what nickname?

9. Who was the new greeter at Air Canada Centre for the Leafs in 1999?

10. Which president of the Maple Leafs is well known for the award named after him?

ANSWERS 10

1. The Leafs blew a three goal lead in the 3rd period.
2. George Armstrong
3. Kamloops Blazers
4. Alexander Steen
5. Radar
6. Syl Apps
7. Inge Hammarstrom
8. Turk
9. Andy Frost
10. Conn Smythe

QUESTIONS 11

1. Who was in goal when the Leafs captured the 1967 Stanley cup?

2. On February 9, 2000, in their first trade of this century, Toronto sent Mike Johnson, Marek Posmyk, and a few draft choices to Tampa Bay for a package centered around which player who became a popular fixture on the Leafs?

3. Although the Leafs have not excelled at the draft, over the years they have selected a handful of players who would go on to win the championship with other teams. Which of the following Stanley Cup champions was *not* drafted by the Leafs?

4. Which Maple Leafs forward scored the Summit Series clinching goal for Team Canada in 1972 against the USSR?

5. Which elite NHL goaltender was drafted in 1997 with the draft pick that once belonged to the Leafs?

6. Who did the Leafs take with their first pick in 2003?

7. What is Mats Sundin's nickname?

8. In 1951, who scored the winning goal against the Montreal Canadiens to capture the Cup?

9. Who was the first European born Maple Leafs captain?

10. Grinding defenceman Garth Butcher was given what nickname?

ANSWERS 11

1. Terry Sawchuk

2. Darcy Tucker

3. Tyler Seguin

4. Paul Henderson

5. Roberto Luongo

6. John Doherty

7. Weed

8. Bill Barilko

9. Mats Sundin

10. Butch

QUESTIONS 12

1. When Toronto beat Montreal to win the Stanley Cup in 1967, it was the _____ time the Franchise had won the Cup?

2. Who beat out the Leafs in 1999-2000 to stop their run for the cup?

3. Where was Terry Sawchuk traded?

4. In what was purely a depth move to help their AHL affiliate, which player was traded to Toronto in January 2011?

5. Which of these coaches holds the distinction of coaching the Leafs for over 300 regular season games without once leading them to the playoffs?

6. Which one of these star forwards played his entire NHL career (1963-1981) with the Maple Leafs, scoring 332 goals?

7. Who did the Maple Leafs defeat in their first game at the ACC in February 1999?

8. Who did the Leafs take with their first pick in 2004?

9. What was Amos Arbour's nickname?

10. Which of the following years did the Maple Leafs won 3 consecutive cups?

ANSWERS 12

1. 13th

2. New Jersey Devils

3. Detroit Red Wings

4. Fabian Brunnstrom

5. Ron Wilson

6. Ron Ellis

7. Montreal Canadiens

8. Justin Pogge

9. Butch

10. 1947, 1948 and 1949

QUESTIONS 13

1. Which of these players was never a Leaf?

2. Legendary Hall Of Fame defenceman Tim Horton was known by what nickname?

3. In the playoffs, who is the highest scoring defenseman for Toronto ending with the 2001 season?

4. Against which team did the Leafs see the most injuries in 1999-2000?

5. What was George Armstrong's nickname?

6. Which popular Leaf was traded to the Colorado Rockies in 1979, in exchange for Pat Hickey and Wilf Paiment?

7. How many times have the Toronto Maple Leafs lost in the Stanley Cup Finals in the 20th Century?

8. What was Norman Armstrong's nickname?

9. In a unique move, Toronto Hall of Famer Ace Bailey asked that his retired Leaf number 6 be taken out of retirement, so that it could be worn by which of the following Leaf stars?

10. Which former Toronto Maple Leaf goaltender had the most points in a game in the 20th century for a goalie?

ANSWERS 13

1. Domenic Hasek

2. Superman

3. Borje Salming

4. Ottawa Sentators

5. The Chief

6. Lanny McDonald

7. 8

8. Red

9. Ron Ellis

10. Jeff Reese

QUESTIONS 14

1. What was Don Ashby's nickname?
2. Which Leaf was nick-named 'Shakey'?
3. Who did the Toronto Maple Leafs pick in the first round at the 1986 Entry Draft?
4. What was Bob Bailey's nickname?
5. Who was the first Leaf to score 100 points in a season?
6. What NHL Trophy has the Maple Leaf Gardens on it?
7. What was Irvine Bailey's nickname?
8. Against which team did Tim Horton play his last game?
9. How many years did the Toronto Maple Leafs play at Maple Leaf Gardens?
10. What was Earl Balfour's nickname?

ANSWERS 14

1. Ants

2. Mike Walton

3. Vincent Damphousse

4. Bashin' Bob

5. Daryl Sittler

6. Conn Symthe

7. Ace

8. Toronto

9. 68

10. Spider

QUESTIONS 15

1. Which Toronto Maple Leaf star had his career abruptly ended in 1934 by a viscous hit from behind, by Bruin Eddie Shore?
2. Who is the only Leaf to win the Selke Trophy in the 20th century?
3. What was Harold Ballard's nickname?
4. Which Maple Leaf defenceman incited a near riot in Boston with a thunderous check on Bobby Orr during a 1969 playoff game?
5. How many seats are there in the Air Canada Centre?
6. What was Bill Barilko's nickname?
7. Which Toronto goalie was given the nickname 'Ulcers'?
8. Who scored the first goal in the Air Canada Centre?
9. What was Aldege Bastien's nickname?
10. Which colourful Leaf stood on the bench and conducted chanting fans with his stick during a home game in 1974?

ANSWERS 15

1. Ace Bailey

2. Doug Gilmour

3. Pal Hal

4. Pat Quinn

5. 18,819

6. Bashin' Bill

7. Frank McCool

8. Todd Warriner

9. Baz

10. Eddie Shack

QUESTIONS 16

1. Which one of these companies was not a sponsor of the Toronto Maple Leafs in the 2002 season?

2. What is Tie Domi's nickname?

3. What Leaf defenceman and right wing won the Calder Trophy in 1947, the same year Gordie Howe broke in with Detroit?

4. Which of the following was a captain for the Toronto Maple Leafs in the 20th century?

ANSWERS 16

1. Labatt

2. The Albanian Assassin

3. Howie Meeker

4. Syl Apps

Manufactured by Amazon.ca
Bolton, ON